Come here, Puss!

By Eve Browne

"Puss! Puss!" said Tilly.

"Come here, Puss."

"Luke," said Tilly.

"Is Puss in the basket?"

"No," said Luke.

"Mum," said Tilly.

"Is Puss on the chair?"

"No," said Mum.

Dad looked for Puss.

Nana looked for Puss.

Pop looked for Puss.

"Puss is here!"
said Tilly.

"Puss is here in the sun,"
said Tilly.